Baby Sleep Guide to Promote Healthy Sleep Habits

Wise Tips and Tricks to Help Your Newborn Sleep Through the Night, Proven Modern Training to Calm Crying Infants for No Cry Nights and a Happy Child

Heidi Oster

© Copyright 2019 - All rights reserved.

The content contained within this book may not be reproduced, duplicated or transmitted without direct written permission from the author or the publisher.

Under no circumstances will any blame or legal responsibility be held against the publisher, or author, for any damages, reparation, or monetary loss due to the information contained within this book. Either directly or indirectly.

Legal Notice:
This book is copyright protected. This book is only for personal use. You cannot amend, distribute, sell, use, quote or paraphrase any part, or the content within this book, without the consent of the author or publisher.

Disclaimer Notice:

Please note the information contained within this document is for educational and entertainment purposes only. All effort has been executed to present accurate, up to date, and reliable, complete information. No warranties of any kind are declared or implied. Readers acknowledge that the author is not engaging in the rendering of legal, financial, medical or professional advice. The content within this book has been derived from various sources. Please consult a licensed professional before attempting any techniques outlined in this book.

By reading this document, the reader agrees that under no circumstances is the author responsible for any losses, direct or indirect, which are incurred as a result of the use of information contained within this document, including, but not limited to, — errors, omissions, or inaccuracies.

Contents

Introduction _____ 1

Chapter 1:
What You Need to Know About Baby Sleep _____ 3

Chapter 2:
Bedtime Problems and How to Can Fix Them _____ 15

Chapter 3:
What Is Normal Sleeping Behavior _____ 19

Chapter 4:
Tools You Need for Success _____ 29

Chapter 5:
Develop a Sleep Schedule _____ 45

Chapter 6:
Sleep with Assistance Plan (SWAP) _____ 51

Chapter 7:
Sleep Learning Independence Plan (SLIP) _____ 65

Chapter 8:
If Night Waking Starts to Happen Again? _____ 79

Chapter 9:
How to Handle Naptime Troubles _____ 87

Chapter 10:
Common Setbacks _____ 91

Conclusion _____ 101

Baby Sleep
GUIDE TO PROMOTE
Healthy Sleep Habits

Wise Tips and Tricks to Help Your Newborn Sleep Through the Night, Proven Modern Training to Calm Crying Infants for No Cry Nights and a Happy Child

HEIDI OSTER

Heidi Oster

Introduction

The following chapters will discuss everything that you need to know to help get your baby to sleep at night. There are many parents who are ready to get their baby to fall asleep at night. Sure, they love the cuddles and all the relaxing time with their baby, but they don't like having the baby attached to them all the time. They want to be able to do things around the house, take a bath, or even get to bed without having an upset baby every night of the week.

This guidebook is going to discuss some of the different sleep training methods that you can use to help put your baby to sleep at night. Some will require a bit of assistance from the parent and others follow the cry it out method to help baby get to sleep at night. Each of these methods can be effective; you just need to find the one that works the best for you and for your baby.

In addition to discussing the different sleep training methods that are inside this guidebook (even though that is the meat and potatoes and the main reason you are here), we will discuss some of the other things you need to know about your baby and how they sleep. We will look at some of the different guidelines for how babies sleep at different ages; some great tools that can help you get the baby to sleep and keep them asleep, and even some of the common problems you may encounter when you try to sleep train.

Every parent loves their baby, but they also love to sleep as well. Use this guidebook to help you get that baby to sleep safely and independently.

Chapter 1:
What You Need to Know About Baby Sleep

Having a new baby can be an exciting time. You went through the whole pregnancy excited to have the baby, and now that you have that little bundle of joy and have learned their little personalities, you are on cloud nine. But now that you are taking care of your new baby and perhaps their siblings as well, you are tired and worn out. And if your baby has trouble falling asleep at night, then this can make the exhaustion even worse.

This book is meant to help out parents who have a challenging baby or child who just won't go to sleep. This can be children who have their days and nights mixed up, the ones who will only sleep when they are in their parent's arms, or those who just have trouble sleeping altogether. Let's take a look at some of the things that you need to know to get started with baby sleep training and help you to finally get the baby to sleep through the night.

Things I Need to Know to Start

Before we get in-depth about sleep training and how to do it on your baby, there are a few truths that we need to know about. These truths are going to be fundamental to helping us know what is going to happen when we start on sleep training. There are often a lot of misunderstandings about sleep training, so having these out of the way can make sleep training so much easier.

You are the best parent to your child. Yes, parenting can be hard, and at times, when the child is awake in the middle of the night, you may feel like a failure. Just remember that you aren't a failure. You are amazing. No one can do better for your child than you, and your child is so lucky that you are their parent.

You and your partner will probably get into many fights about your child and how well they sleep. This is just something that happens when you get tired and frustrated. You may have one night where you are whisper-fighting at three in the morning about how you should handle the crying baby. And the next night you will think that your husband is a jerk because they are pretending to sleep in order to deal with whatever is happening with the baby. Everyone can get grumpy when they feel tired. Forgive each other during this time. Someday when the baby is grown up and sleeps through the night, you will laugh about the whole thing.

Babies are not going to outgrow sleep issues. Rather, they grow into them. You may as well get ready for a hard time now. If you get started with it today, this will help you to get sleep later. Your kid won't simply outgrow the sleep issues. They will just get worse unless you teach them the right sleep habits early on.

Remember that sometimes babies won't sleep the way that you want them to simply because they are babies. And for today, that is something that you need to accept because it's as good as it gets. Over time, things will get better so don't despair here.

Helping your child get some healthy sleep habits now is one of the best parenting decisions that you can do for them. As a new parent, there is probably a ton of noise around you about how to be a good parent and how to do this or that. But it all boils down to giving your child all the love you have to give, spend time with them each day, play with them outside, and help them to sleep. If you can handle these few tasks, then you are doing everything right for your child.

And while this guidebook does focus on sleep training, it is important to not become obsessed with the sleep pattern of your child. Sure, getting them on a sleep pattern is important for their health and their development. But if you spend all day, every day focusing on how you will get them to sleep and worrying about whether they are sleeping or not, you will miss out on all the fun stuff that comes with having a baby.

Learning how to get your baby to sleep at night is a process. It is not something that you will be able to do in one night. In fact, you need to be in for the long haul. There may be times when it gets harder before it gets better. But if you persist with the work, and realize that it will get better you will soon be able to get your baby to sleep through the night without all the hassles and all the roadblocks that you are facing now.

Where Should the Baby Sleep?

Hopefully, at this point, you have a plan for where you want to let the baby sleep. Newborns don't always go with the plan that you have in place, so remember that a little flexibility can be important. But have a firm idea and aim for it when the baby is about six months old or so. Some parents like to have the baby sleep well in a crib in their own room, and others may like them to sleep in the same room as the parent.

No matter what your long-term goal is, most babies end up sharing a room with their parents for at least a bit of their first few months. This often makes it easier for parents to hear their babies and can shorten the distance the parent has to travel when it is time to feed the baby. Keep in mind that room sharing and co-sleeping are not the same things.

Babies who spend at least the first few months in a room with their parents actually have a lower incidence of SIDS. This is why it is often recommended for babies between the newborn and six-month stage. And because newborns require quite a bit of night parenting, having the baby nearby can be really convenient for the parent as well.

If it is more convenient for you, or you and the baby will sleep better when the baby is in another room, that is fine as well. Some parents find that they do better when the baby is in their own room. If you are doing this, make sure that you have a crib prepared for the baby, one with tight-fitting sheets, no extra blankets, or toys inside, and that the baby lies down on their back.

The other decision that you will need to make is what kind of sleep-surface you want the baby to be on. Now, you may find that you have some ideas with this, but the baby prefers to go with something else. Let's say that for now, you get the choice and your baby will go wherever you put them!

According to the American Academy of Pediatrics, your baby should only ever sleep in a play yard, bassinet, or crib that meets the CPSC safety standards. However, many parents find that it is hard to get their newborn to sleep well in a crib when they first bring them home. While you should try to put the baby in a crib, some do well with this and may surprise you, and in some, you may find that it doesn't work that well.

Combining crib-sleeping and co-rooming can be a challenge. Most of the time you won't be able to get the crib through the doorway and you would have to take it apart when you are ready to move it. Space limitations in your bedroom can make this difficult as well. This can present a problem. You may want to talk with your pediatrician and see if you can find a safe sleep space that allows the child to sleep well and that can also be put int your room. Something like a portable crib may work best.

A Note About Co-Sleeping
The co-rooming that we have been talking about at this point is when the baby sleeps in the same room as you. Co-sleeping is when the baby sleeps with you in your bed. Sometimes co-sleeping is going to occur all night as a decision by the parent. And other times the baby will fall asleep in their crib (or

another sleeping place), and then join the parents in bed as a last-ditch effort to finally get the baby to sleep in the middle of the night.

There are a lot of different options when it comes to co-sleeping. Some parents choose to co-sleep because they like the convenience, find that the baby sleeps better when nearby, or they like to have the baby physically near them all of the time. This is known as proactive co-sleeping and it will last for the full night. Some parents may choose to just do co-sleeping for naps to make things easier.

There is also reactive co-sleeping. This is when parents didn't want or plan to co-sleep, but when they find the baby won't sleep in another fashion, they resort to this. Or, they may have brought the baby in to breastfeed them and then the baby and the parent fell asleep.

Proactive co-sleeping is something that has brought up a lot of controversy in the United States, but it is a cultural phenomenon. Asian countries exclusively co-sleep with their infants, and sometimes with older children. In fact, up to 59 percent of Japanese parent's co-sleep with their babies. In the United States, this type of co-sleeping is less common and it is estimated that only about 9 percent of families do this.

Many doctors and health professionals recommend that you don't co-sleep with your baby, but there is a growing number of parents who are showing the benefits of co-sleeping and how it can help the parent and the baby develop a strong bond. If you are considering working with co-sleeping, do it only if you are drug-free, don't drink alcohol, and if you don't smoke. And make sure to discuss this matter with your doctor to see if this is a good idea for you and for your baby, and to learn any of the safety measures that you should follow to keep your baby safe during this time.

If you do decide to co-sleep with your baby, some of the rules that you should consider include:

- Do not co-sleep with a baby who is premature.
- Do not co-sleep with pets, other adults that are not the parents, or siblings.
- Parents who smoke should never co-sleep.
- Use a firm bed surface. This means no waterbeds, air beds, or mattress toppers, pillows, blankets, or thick bedding.
- Pull the bed away from the wall and then take the headboard off if you can to reduce any risks of the baby getting trapped between things.
- Never leave the baby alone on the adult bed. No matter how big the bed or small the child, they may be able to roll out sooner than you would think.
- If you can, consider putting the mattress right on the floor to reduce some of the risks.

Sleep Safety Rules

Before we get started on some of the sleeping techniques in this guidebook, it is important to talk about some of the safe sleeping rules. These ensure that once you get the baby to sleep, you are able to keep them safe during the night. Some of the rules that you want to consider include:

Place the Baby on Their Back for Sleeping

In the past, mothers were told that their babies should be placed to sleep on their front. This was because the thoughts at the time were that babies were less likely to choke when they were sick if they were in this position. But according to research that has been done throughout the world, the safest position for a baby is to be put down on their back.

This research has found that the risk of SIDS in your baby will increase six times if they are sleeping on their front. And since there is no rise in choking in babies who sleep on their back, this is a completely safe position for them to sleep in. When you place the baby down in their bed at night, make sure that you make sure they are on their back. If your baby does happen to roll over to their tummy during the night, just gently turn them back over again. After they turn six months old and are able to turn onto their tummies and then back again on their own, then it is fine to let your baby stay on their tummies if they happen to roll over at night.

Keep the Bed Clear for Your Baby

When you lay the baby down to sleep for the night, make sure that you don't have anything in the crib with this. Don't have any bulky or soft bedding, pillows, a cot bumper, duvets, quilts, or soft toys inside. All of these things can cause a suffocation risk, and with a bumper, there is also a strangulation risk involved as well. It is especially important to avoid using pillows in the crib because studies done by different groups, including the Lullaby Trust, show that a pillow alone could double the risk of SIDS for your baby.

Some of the things that you can do to help make sure the bedding around your baby is as safe as possible are the following:

- Take any blankets and sheets that you are using and tuck them in as firmly as possible. Place your baby with the feet at the foot of the bed so that they aren't able to wiggle down and get the sheets over their heads.

- Use a sleeping bag. These are going to keep the baby warm and will ensure that they won't need any blankets or sheets in the first place.

Remember that it is perfectly safe to swaddle your baby, as long as you make sure you do it properly. Don't swaddle above the shoulders and don't do the swaddle too tightly. Once the baby is able to roll over, when they reach about four months old, you should stop using this practice.

Don't Allow the Baby to Get Hot

While it is in our instincts to wrap up the baby as much as possible, letting the baby get too hot could increase the risks of SIDS. This is especially important to remember any time that it is cold outside. Babies actually need a cooler room than most people might assume. The recommended safe temperature for the baby at night is between 61 and 68 degrees.

You don't want to rely on just how the room feels to you. Make sure to use a room thermometer to make sure. You can also check on the baby to see if they are overheating. Don't check at the feet though because, like adults, the feet can often run much colder than the rest of the body. Look at the tummy or the back of the neck of your baby to see how warm they are.

Keep the House Smoke-Free
This is a safety parenting advice that will start during your pregnancy. There is a huge link between SIDS and parents who smoke. While there isn't definitive evidence out there for this, many groups believe that about 30 percent of sudden infant deaths could be avoided if the mothers didn't smoke when they were pregnant. The best advice that you can follow for this one includes:

- When you find out you are pregnant, make sure to stop smoking and have anyone else around you or around the house stop smoking as well.

- Don't allow anyone to smoke in the same room as the baby.

- Don't allow visitors to your house to smoke in the home. Some parents

- choose to ask visitors not to smoke at all, and some request them to smoke outside.

- Don't take the baby into places that are going to be smoky.

Never Sleep on An Armchair or The Sofa with Your Baby

While you may find at times that it is easy to fall asleep while holding the baby on your sofa, sleeping with the baby can be dangerous because it can increase the risk of SIDS. This is because the baby can slip into the gaps of the cushions of the couch, or the sofa back and the cushions. It is also possible for you to slip down or roll on top of the baby. Many deaths of babies happen because the parent and baby fall asleep on the sofa together.

If you are sitting on the sofa with your baby and feeding them and you are worried that you might fall asleep, then bring out the phone and set an alarm. This will wake you up within a few minutes if you do fall asleep. If you are sitting on the sofa and holding the baby, make sure to set them down in their baby-box, Moses basket, crib, or cot.

Share A Room with The Baby

During the first six months, it is safest for your baby to sleep in a crib or cot in whichever room you are in. According to a 2013 study that was funded by The Lullaby Trust, about 75 percent of the babies who died from SIDS during the day were sleeping in a room all on their own.

The reason that sleeping in the same room with the baby might be that having the parent nearby could have a type of protective effect on the baby. Or maybe having the baby near you allows you to respond to the needs of the baby better. Either way, room sharing with your baby definitely helps reduce the risks of SIDS.

Remember that room sharing and co-sleeping are not the same things. While room sharing is safe, co-sleeping can be unsafe for your baby. You can run the risk of issues with rolling over and on top of the baby while you are sleeping. It is best to let the baby sleep in the same room as you, but make sure they are in their own area to sleep, such as in a bassinet or a crib.

Chapter 2:
Bedtime Problems and How to Can Fix Them

As a new parent, there are a lot of things that you need to pay attention to when it comes to bedtime. You want to ensure that your baby is getting the amount of sleep that they need to be healthy and happy, but if you are struggling with some of the common bedtime problems that other new parents are, this process may be easier said than done. Here are a few of the most common bedtime problems you may be dealing with concerning your little one and the steps you can take to fix them.

The Bedtime Chosen Is Too Late
A late bedtime is one of the challenges that new parents may face. It is going to show up with bedtime battles, waking up often during the night, and an early start to the day. Think of this as "baby is awake too long before bedtime," which means that the baby is going to be overtired. Despite what many parents may think, an overtired baby will have a hard time falling and staying asleep.

If you are struggling with getting your child to fall asleep, it may be time to switch up their bedtime a bit. Even moving it ahead a few minutes each day until it gets to a more reasonable time can make a difference in how well the baby sleeps. If you had a child who fell asleep without any issues and now, they are struggling to sleep, you may have moved bedtime a little early. This is a balancing act and you may have to experiment to find the perfect bedtime for your baby.

The Bedtime Is Inconsistent

Some kids are going to have a bedtime that is really inconsistent. With newborns, you may find that you choose bedtimes based on how the naps went that day so you can make sure they get enough sleep. If the baby took short naps that day, you may move the bedtime to earlier to help them get enough sleep. If they took a long nap, you may let them stay up a little later.

But for kids who are older than 3 months, it is important to lock them into a consistent bedtime. Varying times of going to bed can make it harder for the baby to fall asleep. There have also been studies that show how an inconsistent bedtime can even be associated with a higher rate of a behavioral problem later on.

If your goal is to help your child sleep better at night, then you need to look at your schedule and make some adjustments to bedtime so that this happens as close to the same time as possible every day. Lock this in and keep it there.

The Bedtime Is Too Early for The Baby

Sometimes your baby may go to bed too early. Even though we just talked about the benefits of making sure your baby doesn't go to bed too late, it is still possible that you are picking out a bedtime that is too early. Some of the indicators that you are putting your baby to bed too early include:

- The baby consistently struggles to fall asleep at bedtime. Most babies and even older kids will be fast asleep within twenty minutes of going to bed.

- Your child is routinely awake and won't go back to sleep for longer periods of time in the middle of the night. Some babies will do this on occasion, but when it happens all the time, you may need to reconsider the bedtime.

- The bedtime doesn't have a long enough stretch of awake-time ahead of it. If the baby went down for a nap about an hour before bedtime, they probably won't be ready to go to bed for the night.

- Your child has a healthy amount of sleep, which is between ten to twelve hours at night but wakes up too early for you, then it may be time to push bedtime back an hour.

If you are getting a combination of these symptoms, then it may be time to make the bedtime a little later each night. Start by doing fifteen minutes later each day until you get to the bedtime that works the best for you. If you do this for seven nights in a row and you don't really see an improvement, then it is fine to go back to the original bedtime that you had.

Bedtime Stinks

Once your child is no longer a newborn, the bedtime in your home should be your favorite time of the day. You may enjoy all the cuddles, the cute pajamas, and the quiet that you are going to get when they go to sleep can be so welcome for many parents. But sometimes, figuring out what is causing your baby to stay awake and not fall asleep can evade you. There are many ways that bedtime can stink for a new parent including:

- It takes ages to soothe the baby and get them to sleep.

- You have to go back and forth into your baby's room a million times before they fall asleep.

- Your child is up so late most nights that you pretty much go to bed right after they do.

- Bedtime is a long stretch of limit-testing cries for more. This could be for more books, kisses, hugs, water, and so on.

If this sounds like something that happens at your home, then it is time to figure out why bedtime stinks so bad, and then come up with a good plan to help improve it. The plan that you use will depend on the reason that bedtime is so bad and how old the baby is at the time. The good news is that with some time and patience, and the right plan, you will soon get the baby to sleep through the night.

Chapter 3:
What Is Normal Sleeping Behavior

One of the best things that you can do to help with understanding your baby and the way that they sleep is to know how babies tend to sleep during the different stages of their lives. If you start with sleep training when the baby is too young, you are going to put in a lot of wasted effort. For example, a newborn is not going to get on a regular schedule, no matter how hard you try. But by the time they reach about nine months old, you can get them into a good sleeping pattern. Let's look at the sleep development of different age groups, as your baby gets older.

What Is Normal for A Newborn?
The newborn stage of sleeping is one of the toughest ones for new parents to get through. The baby is often on a sporadic sleep schedule and will not sleep for long periods of time. Newborns are going to sleep in short little bouts, usually ranging from half an hour to four hours, and there won't be much routine in the times they get this sleep. Their sleep time can vary quite a bit. During the first few days, they may sleep between sixteen and eighteen hours each day. By the time they get to four weeks, they average out to

fourteen hours. But this can vary between babies as well. Some need more and some need less.

The time of when adults fall asleep is going to be controlled by their circadian rhythms. This is a physiological change that will follow a regular 24-hour cycle. Many of these can be influenced by how much light exposure we get. For instance, when you expose yourself to some sunlight throughout the day, you are helping the body calibrate its internal clock. Even if you are low on sleep, morning light can make sure that you are alert during the day.

On the other side of things, the absence of light is going to help the body slow down a bit. When darkness falls, your brain is going to interpret this as a signal to start producing melatonin, a hormone that can trigger the body to relax and can make it easier to fall asleep.

It is possible for you to disrupt this process a bit. For example, if you expose yourself to some artificial light sources throughout the evening, especially if they are blue lights, you may confuse the body. But as long as you stick with the program, having light during the day and dark at night, you will usually find your natural rhythm.

However, a newborn is not going to be governed by this strong circadian rhythm. It doesn't necessarily start out this way. In the womb, the newborn fell into the same patterns as the mother. The fetal breathing and heart rates would speed up when the mother was active and then slow down when the mother was sleeping. These changes could see some help from some of the hormones from the mother, especially melatonin.

But after birth, this hormonal connection is broken and it is up to the newborn to develop these circadian rhythms themselves. This is a process that takes time. The baby is not going to be born able to do this, and this can mean a lot of long nights for mom and dad. At about twelve weeks old, the baby will start to show the day and night rhythms due to the fact that they start producing melatonin. This is when they will start to get more of the regular sleep patterns that can help mom and dad get more sleep at night as well.

What Is Normal for Three to Six Months?

When you include the naps and nighttime sleeping, your three to six-month-old will sleep between fifteen and sixteen hours a day. Typically, by the time the baby reaches four months, they are going to develop some more regular patterns when it comes to being asleep and awake and some have been able to drop down to fewer night feedings at that time.

This doesn't mean that it is time to make a really rigid sleep program for your four-month-old. If your baby has developed some sleep patterns that are steady and fit in well with the schedule that you want, that is fine. Go ahead and encourage these a bit. But if you want to make sure that your baby is able to sleep longer at one time and have more regular hours, then this is a good time to introduce a bit of sleep training.

Remember that while there are some generalizations, each baby has their own unique developmental schedule. Observe how your child reacts to sleep training, and if they don't seem ready, then you can wait a bit and try it again in a few weeks. At some point though, somewhere between four and six months, most babies will be able to sleep through at least a few hours at a time. Once this happens, you will feel more relieved because you as the parent will be able to get in a few full sleep cycles as well.

Some babies who did well with sleeping through the night early on in this period may find that they go through a sleep regression or a period of time when they start waking up every few hours again. This is just temporary and will usually end, as long as you keep with your regular bedtime routine as much as possible. The baby may be growing, may be practicing some of their new skills in their sleep and waking up, or becoming more socially aware, and cries because they want your company.

This is a good time to start setting up some good sleeping habits with your baby. You don't have to keep it completely rigorous at this time. But having your own sleep schedule in place can make it much easier for you to get the baby to sleep when you want later on.

What Is Normal for Six to Nine Months?

A typical six to nine-month-old is going to sleep between fourteen to fifteen hours a day. This is split up between their naps and their nighttime sleep though, so don't be surprised if they sleep too much during the day and they aren't able to sleep at night. Many times, by this age, the baby is able to sleep for much longer stretches of time, which can mean some relief for the parents at night. Many of the babies in this age group are going to consolidate their naps down to about two, one in the morning and one in the afternoon.

This is also the period when most babies start sleeping through the night, though there will be some babies who don't yet. If your baby is able to sleep for about eight hours or a little more during the night, it means that they are learning how to settle back to sleep, and it is a great sign that you are raising a good sleeper.

Don't fret too much if your baby isn't sleeping straight for eight hours. Many babies are still waking up for some feedings during this stage. Many are ready for night weaning at this time if you choose to do it. Many times, when a baby wakes up during this time, it isn't because they are hungry. They may wake up for brief periods of time during the night. Some babies wake themselves up more and need help getting back to sleep. Others are able to fall right back to sleep without making a noise.

While major developmental milestones during this time could be partly to blame for the issues with sleeping during this time, another issue to watch out for is teething pain. If you suspect that the baby is waking up because of their teeth during this time, they may just need a little extra cuddling to help them get into a deep sleep.

Each child is going to be different. There are some babies who will be great sleepers with very little work from their parents. And then there are some babies who will need some extra time and patience from their parents to get into a good sleep schedule. And if you have big life events, illness, or traveling during this time, you will just need to roll with the changes and know that your baby may get off their sleep schedule for a bit. Maintaining a steady schedule can help get them back on track faster.

What Is Normal for Nine Months to One Year?
Most nine to twelve months old is going to sleep about fourteen hours a day, including two naps that are about one to two hours at a time based on your schedule. Some pediatricians do notice that babies this age will have different sleep patterns during this time. This could be because the baby is reaching some new milestones during this time or because they get more calories from solid foods, so they can sleep for longer.

If you haven't been able to get the baby to fall into a sleep pattern at this time yet, then now is the time to get started with it. These sleep training methods can do a great job at helping your baby get to sleep more easily, sleep for longer periods of time during the night, and can give you a break because they get on more regular hours. If you have trouble getting them on a schedule during this time, it is time to use some of the different sleep techniques we will discuss in this guidebook.

If your baby is able to sleep for about nine to ten hours at a time during the night, then it means the baby knows how to settle back into sleep when they wake up and it is a sign that you already have a good sleeper. At this time, it is time to do night weaning because most babies are not going to wake up as much at night due to hunger.

There are some babies who run into trouble with waking up at night and not falling asleep. These often show up with some major milestones in motor and cognitive development. And for some babies, it could be a sign of separation anxiety. You can go in and help calm them down a little bit, and usually, this is enough to get them back to sleep.

During this age, you need to stick with your consistent bedtime routine, keep the baby on a regular schedule as much as possible, and make sure the baby has plenty of chances to fall asleep all on their own.

What Is Normal for Toddlers?

If you do not work with your child at a young enough age, it is possible that they will suffer from sleep problems even when they reach older than one year of age. Knowing what to expect when your baby turns into the next stage of being a toddler can make it easier to come up with a sleep schedule that works well for them as well.

Most toddlers are going to be early risers. This is just how their system is set up so don't be upset if they come in to wake you up between six and seven in the morning. Whenever they wake up though is fine, as long as they get enough sleep and their rising time fits into the schedule that works for your family. If your child seems to be sleepy most of the morning, or they want a nap after only being up for a few hours, then they may need to go to bed earlier at night or be sent back to bed for another round of rest in the morning.

If your toddler wakes up around seven in the morning, you will want to aim for a nap around 9:30 in the morning. But as they grow, they will phase out of this nap time. Many one-year-olds to eighteen months old will start to phase out of this nap time, and that is fine. Just make sure that they have a little time for being quiet in the morning. Spend this time playing independently, listening to stories on CDs, or looking at books. They don't have to be completely asleep during this time, but the quiet time can help the child recharge for active periods during the day.

If your toddler needs it, or if they don't take that first-morning nap, then you will need to give them another round of rest after a good lunch. Most of the time, getting them to nap between 1:30 and 2 in the afternoon are the best. Make sure that the nap stays under two hours. If the child does end up napping too late in the afternoon, it may interfere with their ability to sleep at night. You can alter this nap schedule to fit your needs. Some kids may need to take a nap a little earlier, but make sure that they are getting this rest time in the afternoon.

The routine that you see from one home to another will vary; but generally, a toddler is going to fall asleep sometime between six and eight at night. This is plenty of time for the toddler to get their twelve hours of sleep at night and then they can still be up for a family breakfast and have time for the family at night. Try to schedule bath time for six at night and then give them some time to relax before a bedtime at seven. Or you can adjust this to work for your family. Just make sure that there is some winding down time before the baby has to head to bed.

Baby Sleep Guide to Promote Healthy Sleep Habits

Chapter 4:
Tools You Need for Success

No matter how hard you try, you can't make the baby sleep or do anything else for that matter. But while you can't force the baby to fall asleep, you do have some resources at your disposal that can help you encourage your baby to sleep. The baby has to be tired, or be ready for bed, but you can utilize some tools to help you to encourage the baby to reach that stage and get them out for some good shut-eye.

There are a variety of tools that you can use that will help your child to sleep. Some of them are going to be really effective, but others are going to really cause more problems than they are able to solve. You may find that your baby reacts better to some of these tools compared to others, and sometimes it takes a little bit of experimenting to get results. The tools that we are going to discuss in this chapter are going to help encourage sleep for your baby in ways that you aren't going to regret down the road.

These tools will safely and significantly encourage your baby to fall asleep, and can also help them stay asleep. Some of the criteria for tools to be listed in this guidebook include:

- It needs to elevate the degree of soothing that the baby gets helping to increase the odds that your baby will fall asleep and then stay asleep. While you can't make your baby fall asleep, you can certainly make it hard for them to stay awake.

- It functions for the whole time your child is sleeping. Anything that is on a timer will not count here because the timer can turn off the device.

- It can work without much parental involvement. For example, we are not going to recommend putting the baby in a car and driving them around. Sure, this gets most babies to fall asleep, but until self-driving cars come around, it includes a ton of parental involvement.

- The device is not you. Sure, you may be able to hold your baby and get them to sleep, but you are probably tired of doing that. None of these techniques are going to involve you as the parent getting the baby to sleep.

- It is something that you can wean the baby off of in the future in a gentle way. This means that you get the benefit of using the tool without worrying about whether you will have to fight to break them off it in the future.

Keep in mind that not all of the tools we are going to discuss will work for all ages. The ones that we choose are specific for babies to help you finally get that much-needed rest with them. Some will work until the baby is older, but don't be surprised if they kind of outgrow it.

A Note About You as The Sleeping Tool

One note here is to realize that we are not trying to make nursing, cuddling, or holding the baby to sleep a bad thing. And when you have a newborn, the only place you may be able to get them to sleep is on you. This actually gives you a lot of freedom and flexibility when they are first born to go out and meet friends and get out of the house.

With a newborn, cuddling the baby to sleep or nursing them to sleep may be the only thing that works for those high-need newborns. And that is not a bad thing. Nor are we spending time here saying that you should forgo the joys of having a little infant sleeping in your arms. If this is what you find the easiest when they are brand new, then go ahead and get the cuddles as much as you want.

What we are talking about here is a baby who has reached past the newborn stage and is much older, but who still fusses whenever they are put down. Doing this too much and for too long can lead to some troubles such as:

- Teaching the baby that sleeping with you or on you is the only way that they can fall asleep. This is not something that you can sustain over the long term.

- Making it hard to convince a baby who is older and who have spent their whole life sleeping on you that sleeping somewhere else is a good thing and this can be a challenge. This is how parents become stuck sleeping with a baby for many months.

- Creating a really unfeasible sleep or nap arrangement with older children.

- Unsafe sleep situations: An infant who is asleep on your lap on the couch when you are wide awake is not a big deal. But if you fall asleep with them there, it can be unsafe.

- The absence of any transition strategy to help get the baby to sleep independently.

So, while it is just fine to take that newborn and cuddle and hold them tight, but mindful that the goal here is to gradually foster safe, sustainable, and independent sleep. And for most families, this is the process of establishing sleep that doesn't always involve you.

White Noise

Now that we have looked at some of the basics that come with sleep for the baby, and the importance of not becoming a human mattress yourself, it is time to look at some of the best tools that can help your baby to fall asleep. The first option is known as white noise. This is often the most effective, easiest to implement and the least expensive sleep method for your baby.

There are some parents who don't want to invest in the machine or who feel that their baby will become addicted to this kind of noise. But this just puts them at a disadvantage because white noise is really so great for your baby and getting them to sleep. Plus, it is really easy to work with.

White noise can help reduce some of the stress that your baby may feel. What would a baby get stressed out about? Just about everything in this new and big world. They may be stressed because they are so tired, the world has a lot of stimulation, or because mom and dad are trying to put them to sleep without holding them. White noise can create a new safe space for the baby simply by blocking out all that extra stimulation.

White noise can actually help your baby to sleep. In fact, a good source of white noise is able to help the baby fall asleep easier and even keeps them asleep longer. This is because many babies have a sleep arousal period which happens between ever twenty to forty-five minutes. Some babies are not able to fall back to sleep after this arousal, so that means sleep time is over. White noise helps the baby to navigate around these arousals so they get some better sleep and it can block out any noise that keeps the baby awake.

Using a source of white noise can help your baby cry less. Most people throughout the world will use a type of shushing noise to help babies calm down. The white noise can help do this for you if you use it properly. The key is that the white noise needs to be louder than the crying.

In a recent study, it was suggested that babies who had a fan in their room were actually at a lower risk of SIDS compared to other babies. Nobody is quite sure why the fan seems to help. It could be due to the circulating air so the baby isn't rebreathing the same air that they exhaled. But it could do more with the noise that the fan makes. White noise, including that which comes from the fan, is able to reduce active sleep, which is the state of sleep where SIDS is the most likely to occur.

White noise can even help you as a parent fall asleep. If you happen to have your newborn sleeping in the same room as you, which is recommended for the first six months, you will find that they make a lot of noise that can keep you awake. They kick around, grunt, snort, fart, and make a lot of other noises. When you bring the white noise into your room, this can help to mask some of these small sounds so you are able to sleep better.

So, with all of these benefits, you may be curious about how you are going to use it to help your baby fall asleep. You can choose to purchase a white noise generator if you choose, but you don't have to. There are many white noise apps that are available on your tablet or phone. A clock radio that is set to static can do the trick as well. Sometimes using an air purifier or humidifier will make enough noise to do this.

When you have the device you want to use, turn the volume up so it is around 50 decibels, or about the level of someone taking a shower if you are standing in the bathroom with them. This shouldn't be uncomfortably loud. If you notice that it is bothering you a bit, then it is too loud. Leave this white noise in the same area where the baby will sleep and make sure that it is not going to turn off. Only use the white noise when the baby is asleep. When they are awake, you want to expose your baby to things like life, music, and speech.

Due to a rat study that was done in 2003, many people are worried about using a white noise machine to help their babies fall asleep. Researchers from the University of California published a study at this time where baby rats were raised in a sound deprivation chamber. In this chamber, they were exposed to loud and unceasing white noise the whole time they were "children." These baby rats then grew up to be kind of weird.

Because of this study, many parents are worried that using white noise is going to ruin their children. However, moderate use of the white noise, just when the baby is sleeping, is just fine and there is no evidence to suggest otherwise. If you are still concerned, you can always talk with your pediatrician to help you feel more comfortable before using this tool.

Swaddling

The next tool that you may want to consider using is swaddling. This is actually one of the oldest soothing techniques that have been used for thousands of years. It is actually shown to help babies sleep better. There are many reasons to consider swaddling your baby.

The first benefit is that swaddling can help your baby to cry less. In fact, one study found that swaddling reduced the crying rate by 28 percent. This is especially true during the first two months of the baby's life when they are more difficult to soothe.

Swaddling can also help your baby sleep longer and better. Swaddling will prevent the newborn from startling themselves awake with random arm movements when they are asleep. Newborns are sometimes able to wake themselves up accidentally by hitting themselves in the face. Swaddling can help reduce this risk.

Swaddling can help reduce the incidence of SIDS in some cases. Some of the evidence that shows how swaddling can reduce the SIDS risks in your baby include:

- Some studies show that there is a decreased amount of SIDS associated with babies sleeping swaddled on their backs.

- Parents who choose to swaddle their babies are more likely to lay that baby down on their backs.

- Although these babies sleep better, they are more arousable when exposed to noise.

- A retrospective eight-year study that looked at SIDS and infants who were swaddled found that there were no significant risks when the baby was swaddled and left on their backs.

- Sleeping while swaddled is able to hinder the ability of the baby to flip over on their stomach, a position that has been associated with SIDS.

- Swaddling can make it hard for a newborn to accidentally cover their face or their heads with the bedding.

Baby swaddling is almost like a lesson in origami. There are many different ways to do it and often the right way is whichever method you would prefer. You have been successful with swaddling your baby when the arms don't pop out when you are done.

Swaddling the baby with their arms right down at the side is often the most efficient because it is much harder for the baby to break out when their arms are straight. However, there are some babies who prefer to have their arms bent in the swaddle so you may need to experiment with it a bit. Either way, the successful swaddling technique is when the blanket is snug enough that the baby isn't able to wiggle about a lot but still loose enough that you can get two fingers in there.

The focus of swaddling should be on the upper body. The benefits come from keeping the arms as immobile as possible and close to the body. There aren't really any benefits to swaddling the lower body and doing it too tightly could result in hip dysplasia in the body.

Remember that no matter how good you get at swaddling; your little wiggly baby may be able to get out of it. If you find that your baby is just too good at getting out no matter how hard you work, there are some swaddle blankets out there that come with Velcro, which can make the process easier, especially when you are in the dark.

In addition, some babies are going to cry or fuss when they are being swaddled. This is a negative response to the whole process of being swaddled. This doesn't mean that the baby doesn't like swaddling or that they won't sleep better when they are swaddled. Don't let all that complaining fool you because they may really like it, they may have gotten used to what you are doing there and don't want to go to sleep.

Before you decide to start swaddling your baby, there are a few safety concerns you need to pay attention to include:

- Never lay the baby down on their stomachs when they are swaddled. Sleeping face down can increase the risk of SIDS by twelve times when the baby is swaddled. Always lay them on their backs.

- Let other people know the safety rules about swaddling if they are going to do it.

- When your baby has mastered the skill of flipping onto their stomachs, then you should stop swaddling altogether.

- Don't let the baby overheat. No matter what you are doing, swaddling or not, or what time of year, you want to make sure that you are not letting the baby get overheated.

Swaddling can be very comforting to many babies and this is a practice that has been done throughout the world for many generations. It can be a great way to make your baby comfortable and to get them to fall asleep much easier for you.

Using A Pacifier

A pacifier is a tool that a lot of people shy away from because they fear the baby will become addicted to it and it will be impossible to get rid of the habit. It can be hard, in the beginning, to get the baby to take the pacifier and you may have to try out a bunch of them in order to get the baby to take one. Then there are always issues with wondering whether the pacifier is going to hinder your efforts to nurse, although most of these myths have been debunked. And after some time, you have to figure out how to get the baby to give up the pacifier.

However, it is worth it in many cases. Babies have a natural urge to suck on something, especially when they are sleeping, and the pacifier can help with this. Some of the reasons that you may want to consider using a pacifier for your baby include:

- Sucking on the pacifier while they fall asleep has been able to reduce the risk of SIDS.

- Pacifiers are very soothing for the baby. And when they are combined with some of the other soothing techniques, such as white noise and swaddling, they can help improve how well the baby sleeps and can reduce how often they cry.

- Introducing the pacifier after you finish breastfeeding can help meet the need of the baby to suck, while you get a break.

Babies may struggle against things that are essential or helpful for putting them to sleep. Some babies will show a lot of interest in a pacifier, and others won't care about it at all. This can raise a bit of a challenge when it comes to getting the baby to take a pacifier and use it to get them to sleep. But now that we know some of the benefits of using the pacifier, it may be something that you want to experiment with. Some of the things that you should try to get the baby to like their pacifier (if they do end up struggling) include:

- Buy a few different types of pacifiers. Each baby is going to take a different type, and even if one type worked for an older child doesn't mean that it will work for this child. Purchase a few different ones and save the ones that aren't used for later.

- Offer the pacifier at a time when the baby is not hungry. When a baby is starving, they are going to get angry when something that doesn't contain food is put in their mouth.

- Offer the pacifier at a variety of times during the day. Or try it on a different day.

- Experiment with the pull-out technique. This is when you place the pacifier into the mouth of the baby and then flick it a bit like you want to pop it out. The response of the baby is to naturally suck harder. This can help the baby get used to the pacifier and can get them to enjoy it.

- Try adding a little formula or milk to the tip to get them to take it.

Keep in mind that there are some babies who just won't take the pacifier. They may need to have another method to help them soothe at the end of the day. If your baby doesn't enjoy the pacifier, don't try to force it too much.

Baby Swings

Another method that you may try out is a baby swing. Your baby has been swinging sleeping since they were conceived. This swing, which is in the womb, is always rocking the baby around when you are up and moving during the pregnancy, so this is a natural movement that they are used to. This is why it shouldn't come as a surprise that your baby likes to swing and will fall asleep better when swinging. They like the movement which is why they fall asleep in the swing, in a rocking chair, and in the car. You can use this love of motion to help you get your baby to sleep.

Baby swings are a fantastic option because they provide you with three key elements when you are trying to get the baby to sleep. First, there is a consistent rocking motion that is similar to what the baby finds when they are in the womb providing the soothing that the baby is used to and sees as a natural condition for sleep.

Second, even when these swings are fully reclined, they will still make sure the baby is slightly upright. Many babies have a valve at the top of their stomach which is undeveloped still. This means that in some cases, their food, such as the formula or milk, will be pushed up. Sleeping inclined a little bit can help keep food inside the stomach. And unlike the popular crib wedges, which can be dangerous and can cause SIDS, these swings have some baby straps that will keep your baby in place.

And the number one benefit of using these crib swings is that they will help the baby learn how to gradually fall asleep all on their own.

One thing to note here is that the AAP or the American Academy of Pediatrics position on SIDS recommends against babies sleeping anywhere except on their back in an unadorned modern crib. They are against things like swings, pack and plays, bassinets, and any form of co-sleeping. Your overall goal should be for your baby to sleep as much as possible in a crib because this is considered the safest sleep area possible.

That does not mean you can't use the swing to help you out. Many parents will place the baby in the swing so they can fall asleep, being there and watching the whole time. Then, after the baby has had time to fall asleep and self-soothe for a bit, they will move the baby over to a crib and leave them in the safe sleeping arrangement, perhaps with some white noise to help.

However, there are some parents who find that their baby just won't fall asleep in the crib no matter what. They may try the white noise, the rocking, the swing, and everything else. But as soon as they lay the baby down, that baby is awake and crying again. If you are running into troubles getting the baby to sleep, discuss whether a baby swing is good for your baby with your pediatrician.

Most parents will choose to experiment with this baby swing at naptime. This makes it easier for you to watch how things go since you will be awake during this time. You can keep an eye out on the baby. This works for many parents who find that their baby sleeps just fine at night but struggles to stay asleep during the day for nap time.

Some of the steps that you can take to ensure your baby falls asleep when using the swing include the following:

- Put the swing in the area where your baby tends to sleep the most often. This could be in your room or somewhere near their crib.

- Use the right kind of white noise. This helps the baby fall asleep and can mask any of the noises that come from the swing.

- Set up the baby monitor so that you can hear what is going on with the swing.

- Never put the baby into the swing without having all the straps on.

- Begin by putting the swing on the highest speed that you are comfortable with. Once the baby is comfortable and is able to routinely sleep in the swing, you can then go through and experiment a bit with the speed.

- Consider swaddling. Most babies who use a swing are going to be swaddled, but this is not a requirement.

- To start, see if the baby is able to fall asleep all on their own in the swing. If this works, then you win! If it doesn't work (and it won't for all babies), you may need to use a few other techniques to help you out.

If the baby struggles, you can try a few of these options:

- Put something that smells the same as a mom in the swing next to them. This can be a toy or even the shirt that mom wore all day.

- Consider nursing and feeding the baby and rocking them fully to sleep. Then put them into the swing and let them sleep there.

All of these methods can be great tools to ensure that your baby is going to fall asleep at night. Some parents find that they need to use a combination of these techniques to get their baby to sleep. The trick here is to mess around until you find a method that works for you and that will help your baby fall asleep.

Chapter 5:
Develop a Sleep Schedule

Now it is time to talk about setting up a sleep schedule for your baby. This is another tool that you can use which is foundational to how effective all the tools we discussed in the other chapter will be. If you ever try to put your baby to sleep when they are too tired or not tired enough, you are going to end up with a lot of hassle when you try to get the baby to sleep. Most of the tools that we have talked on are about how to get your baby to finally fall asleep. But now we are going to talk more about when to get the baby to go to bed.

Even if a baby is tired, they are not going to just nod off when they need to sleep. In fact, most will stay awake far past when they need to fall asleep, and they will easily get fussy and angry the longer they go. When they are awake for too long, many babies are going to get crabby and can be difficult to soothe. Even worse, if you let the baby stay up too long, it can impact their sleep hormones and their stress hormone production which can make it harder for them to sleep in the first place.

Then the problem can go the other way as well. If the baby hasn't been up long enough, then they aren't going to be tired enough to actually fall asleep.

If their nap goes too late in the afternoon, for example, and then you try to put them to bed too early, they may get mad when you try to put them down and they aren't tired.

This is why having a sleep schedule, or at least as close to a schedule as you can, can ensure that your baby will get enough sleep, but won't fight because you are putting them down too often. But this brings up the question on how I will know when it is time to get the baby to sleep. If you are lucky, the baby will tell you. You just need to pay attention to what they are telling you to catch it.

Signs That Your Baby Is Tired

Some babies are going to seem really happy, no matter how long they have been awake. Some will seem fine, and then all of a sudden, they will have a major breakdown out of nowhere. Other babies are going to show you some great signals when they are feeling tired and you can catch them before a meltdown starts to happen. Each baby is different and you need to learn what signals they will send off. Some of the signals that the baby is likely to show off when they start to feel tired includes:

- Yawning.

- Blinks that are done in slow motion.

- Rubbing their eyes.

- Seems like they are interested in eating, but they won't eat anything when the food is offered to them.

- They make movements that are more jerky than usual.

- They stop making eye contact with you.

- They start to lose interest in activities or toys.

- They cry for a new reason at all.

- They start to get fussy.

Tired toddlers and preschoolers are often going to take this to another level. They are more likely to have some tantrums and can get physical, such as throwing and grabbing things or even hitting. Even older children and teenagers can have some signs of being tired, even though they are less likely to show these outward signs of being overtired.

The hardest part about some of these sleepy signs is that most babies are really unreliable about giving them. Or, which happens more often than not, by the time the baby starts to exhibit these signs of being tired, they have reached the point of being overtired. This is why it is so important to keep one eye on how your child is behaving, and the other eye on the clock. If you have gotten them on a good sleeping schedule, you will be able to predict when the child will start to be tired and can take the right precautions to get them to bed before things start to explode.

How long your child is able to stay awake comfortably can depend on a variety of factors, including their age and temperament. And then there are days when, even though you have figured out a sleeping schedule with them, it seems like they are able to throw themselves out of it and nothing will appease them. This is perfectly normal and in fact, it is something that you should just prepare for at some point. If there are ever some big life changes, a change in the schedule, or if you travel with your children, then this can throw off their sleep schedule for that time period as well.

This is a big experiment to find out what works for your child. What works for a nap schedule in one family may not work that well for your family. And you may find that each child is going to react to their sleep schedule in a different manner. Some kids may be more of night owls and like having later naps so they can stay up later, and others may like to get up earlier and get to bed at a decent time so they can do it.

Of course, remember that the timing of naps can make a big difference as well. If you put the baby down for an early nap, and then expect them to stay up until late without any other naps, then you are going to end up with a very grumpy baby. However, if you put the baby down for a late nap and then expect them to go to bed at an early hour, you are going to have a baby who is not happy that you are trying to put them to bed early. You need to make sure that there are at least a few hours, but not too many hours, between the last nap and bedtime to make it easier to get your baby to sleep.

It is fine to take your child's lead here. Just make sure that they are getting the recommended number of hours of sleep so that they don't get overly tired and they can grow and develop properly. Over time, you will be able to get the child on a steady schedule with their own circadian rhythm, and bedtime won't be as big of a hassle.

Baby Sleep Guide to Promote Healthy Sleep Habits

Chapter 6:
Sleep with Assistance Plan (SWAP)

Now, we have spent some time looking at some of the best sleep assistance plans to get that baby to sleep. Sometimes, just using a few of the tools that we discussed before won't be enough to get that baby to sleep. You may need to come up with a plan of attack to help get them comfy and into bed. The methods that we are going to talk about in this guidebook are going to be no cry methods.

While there are many people out there who are proponents of the cry it out methods, these are not always the best choice to go with. Studies have shown that the crying out method can be bad on the baby, causing anxiety and many other conditions. These crying it out methods can also be hard on the parents who have to listen to the crying and can't go in to help. Plus, for all that pain and suffering, the crying it out methods is often not that effective.

We are going to focus on easy no-cry methods that will help to get baby to sleep through the night, without any of the issues that can come with the crying it out method. And the first method we are going to take a look at is known as SWAP, or the sleep with assistance plan.

When Is the Best Time to Teach My Baby to Sleep?

While it may seem crazy, there is the easiest time to teach the baby to sleep. Remember that this is the easiest time, not that this is necessarily going to be easy. The rule of thumb that we are going to follow here is the younger the better. This can help the baby develop the skills they need to get to bed at a decent time, to sleep through the night, and to grow and develop the way that they should in the future.

The easiest time for the parent to work on teaching babies to fall asleep all on their own is between the ages of two to four months. If you have a baby in this age range, you may think that this is crazy. For some babies, this process is never easy, so think of this time as the "less horrible time" to sleep train. The process doesn't really get easier when the baby gets older, so you may as well do it when they are younger.

Why is this age range a good one to help teach the baby how to sleep? The first reason is that the baby is young enough that you can still use the tools we already discussed in a safe and effective manner. And when you are trying to convince that four-month-old of yours who likes to fall asleep with nursing that it is time to go to sleep without nursing, these tools can be essential. Trying to remove nursing from sleep can be really hard for a baby and these power tools can help make it easier and they work the best on babies who are a bit younger.

The younger baby is still learning the basics of falling asleep which means they are more malleable especially when compared to older children. An 11-

month old is firmly convinced by that time that there is only one way for them to fall asleep. Convincing them to change those habits can be almost impossible. But the two to four-month-old doesn't know which way there is to fall asleep, and you can be the one to train them.

There are also some fairly predictable sleep setbacks that can occur between four and nine months. These can include separation anxiety, teething, and several sleep regressions. When you start early, you are giving yourself a chance to establish some strong foundation for good sleep in the baby before they run into these potential issues.

Teaching the Baby to Sleep Using the Fundamentals

Teach your child to sleep on their own. This means that you need to introduce the right sleep associations and new techniques to help them get a better quality of sleep. This also means that you will be teaching them a new way to fall asleep compared to what they may have done in the past. We will look at several different techniques that you can use that fit under the category of sleeping with assistance and you can choose the one that you think will work the best with your little one or the one that works the best with your current family schedule. However, any effort to teach the baby to sleep should be based on a solid foundation that will include the following:

- Start out with a bedtime.

- If you don't already have one for your baby, then now is the time to set one. You can pick the bedtime that works the best at your home; just make sure to get one set up.

- Have a bedtime that is age-appropriate and consistent.

- There are lots of guidelines on when to get the child to sleep based on when you get up in the morning and what age the child is. Pick out that bedtime and stick with it, even on the weekends.

- Have a bedtime routine.

- It doesn't have to be a very long bedtime routine, just long enough to signal to the brain that it is time for that child to go to bed. Twenty to thirty minutes is usually long enough. You can give them a warm bath, brush their teeth, and read a few stories before sending them off.

- Keep the room dark.

- You want to make sure the room your baby is sleeping in can be kept dark. A lot of light can distract the baby and may even mess with their own circadian rhythms.

SWAPS to Help Your Baby Fall Asleep Without You

Now it is time to take a look at some of the sleeping plans that you can try with your baby. The SWAPs are nice because they will generally involve a more gradual approach to getting your baby to sleep, will require a lot of parental involvement, and can take a bit longer to implement. But even though they do take longer and need more involvement from you, they are very successful for most babies and you will be happy with spending this time. Let's take a look at the different approaches and what they all mean!

More Soothing

The first method we are going to look at is the more soothing method. This is a method that works well for babies who are under four months of age or ones who are older and have high-needs. It can also work for babies who have a lot of reflux that tends to keep them up.

As we discussed before, younger babies are going to need a lot more soothing to help them settle to sleep at night. Especially when it comes to a newborn, their default source of soothing will be you. They will fall asleep on your lap while you wear them during nursing, and everywhere else that they are close to you. While cuddling with your baby can be nice and we all enjoy doing it, we do need to have some time to take care of older children, work, or do other things without a baby attached. Having a baby who refuses to sleep for more than twenty minutes if they are not held by you can become a problem. The same can happen with children who are high-needs, or who have colic or reflux, and will need more soothing than others.

The solution for this is to provide more soothing. And the best way to do this is to use some of the tools that we discussed in previous chapters. People may choose to skip this step because they believe that independent sleep means that they shouldn't use any tools. Yes, you are trying to move forward and get to a place where the child is able to fall asleep on their own during bed and naps but the goal is not to go without any sleep tools. It's using the right sleep tools and to get them from having to fall asleep on you.

You can use any combination of the tools that we discussed in the other chapters. You may even need to spend some time rocking them to sleep while swaddled, or with a pacifier, and then leaving white noise on to help them fall asleep. While it does require some work from you for a bit, it is worth the time and can be a great way to teach your child to fall asleep. As they get more used to the process, you can work on reducing how long you personally comfort them until you can lay them down in the crib and they fall asleep on their own.

FIO or Fuss It Out
This method will work just fine for most babies who are older than two months of age. This will utilize all of the tools that we talked about, as long as they are age appropriate for your child. You will hold onto the baby, rocking them or letting them sleep on you until the baby is drowsy and calm. Then, while they are still a little bit awake, you will lay them in the crib and walk away.

If the baby is under three months, set a timer for ten minutes. If they are older, you may want to set the timer for a little bit longer. You may hear them grumble a bit and move around, but if you got them to a drowsy state and you have the white noise and other tools present, then you will find they can get themselves to sleep with a few minutes of fussing.

During this stage, you don't want to let them cry it out. If they reach this point, then the tool is not going to help and they will simply wake themselves up. This is why it's important to let the baby get nice and tired and almost asleep before you try it out.

If your baby does fall asleep with this method, this means that you are successful and should be able to continue to use this method with the baby falling asleep all on their own. But if you go through that ten minutes on the timer and the baby hasn't fallen asleep, you have a few decisions to make depending on what is happening and these include:

- The baby is calm, but still awake. If the baby is happy, just leave them alone and see what happens. They may start to get angry, they may fall asleep, or they may just play around for a bit before falling asleep.

- The baby is grumbly and a little fussy, but they are not screaming. The fussy is fine for now. They may just need to adjust a bit before they fall asleep. Wait a bit longer and see what happens.

- The baby starts to scream. You will want to go in and soothe the baby. If you can just walk in and give them their pacifier back or turn the white noise up a bit, and they calm down, then do that. Only pick them up if the crying continues and you can't get them to fall asleep.

While it is possible that your baby will start to cry with this method, it is not a traditional cry it out method. This is a decision to give the baby a brief amount of time to see what will happen if you give them a little space. While it isn't going to work for each baby, some will fall asleep fast if they get removed from the situation. And unlike the cry it out methods, the fuss it out method has a time limit and the parent will go back in. If the baby keeps crying and nothing works, the parents simply go back to their traditional method of sleeping and try something else another night.

The Double Take

This method is best for babies who are under four months old but sometimes kids of older ages will find this beneficial as well. For this one, you are going to soothe your child fully to sleep, picking out any method that works the best for you. When the baby is fully asleep, you can place them in their bed. Once you lay them down, you will wake them up just a little bit. You don't want to wake them up completely, just a little bit. Then allow the baby to fall back into a deep sleep, lying in their own bed.

Some parents have trouble with this one because they don't like the idea that they might undo all the hard work they did by waking the baby back up. But this technique can work because it helps the baby identify that they are in their own bed. Then, when they wake up later in the night at some point, they won't be surprised to be here. Also, make sure to remove any of the unsustainable sleep associations before you wake them up. This means take the pacifier out or make sure you stop the breastfeeding before letting them fall asleep.

You may wonder how awake the baby needs to be when you do this method. You want them to be a little more than eyes barely flutter open. You know that you have gotten the right amount of awake when the baby is grumbling about your behavior.

This is a great technique to work on but remember that it may not be the cure-all to all sleep association challenges. For some babies, it may work, but other times it may not. If you were successful with this double take method with your child for a few nights, and you don't see that there is a big improvement in how well your child sleeps, then this may not be the technique for them and you need to move on and try another one.

Gradual Weaning

This technique is a good one to use with babies who are between two to six months old. As the name suggests, this gradual weaning process is simply taking baby steps to slowly do less of whatever you currently do to help the baby fall asleep. There are a lot of different approaches that you can use to work with gradual weaning, but they all boil down to the ideas that are expressed in this haiku:

- Gradually do less
- Tears and complaints may ensue
- Press on regardless

Some parents may then wonder how they are going to be able to put the baby down awake without the pacifier, sleeping on the chest, nursing, or rocking. They may have spent a lot of time doing these things in the past for their baby and worry about what will happen when they stop.

There are a number of things that you can do here. If the baby is used to falling asleep with a pacifier, consider stopping the use during the day first. Then take it away during short naps, and slowly take it away as they start to fall asleep at night. If the baby likes to be rocked to sleep, you can start by rocking them for shorter amounts of time before putting them in their crib and letting them self-soothe. You can even consider laying them down with some white noise and then rocking the crib a little.

The method that you choose is going to vary depending on what your baby likes to do to fall asleep. Here are examples of how you would do the gradual weaning process if your baby is one who likes to cuddle before they can go to sleep on their own at night

The baby is used to falling asleep while they are snuggled in tight next to you. So, the first step would be to put a small space, about an inch or two, between you and the baby. They may not be too happy about this, and they will try to shift over each time that you move. You may need to use your hand to gently weigh them down and maintain some space. The baby will fuss a bit and the bedtime routine may take a bit longer, but eventually, it will work.

Over time, you decide to expand the distance between you and the baby to maybe six inches. The baby is really not happy about this and tries to move closer. But you are firm and loving at this time. You hold your hand gently on their stomach while singing quietly to them. And after a little bit, she falls asleep.

The next move is when you will put a one-foot gap between you and the baby, and it takes even less time to fall asleep. However, the baby still wakes up frequently at night and you have to spend a lot of time singing with the hand on their belly.

This next step is when the gap between you and your baby is as long as your arm. You still keep your hand on the belly during this time, but you sing or use words, but you end this after three minutes, before pretending to be asleep. Keep pretending to be asleep, even if the baby is fussing or playing around. It will work to get them to sleep.

You are working to create space at bedtime, but now you need to remove your hand from your stomach. The baby may try to move over to you, but you simply must put them back in their spots. You continue to use some words or sing, and within a few minutes, the baby falls asleep.

After this time, you will then want to move the baby to the bed. The baby will probably fuss when you first try to get them to sleep in the bed without any holding. You may need to put your hand on their belly again and sing and talk for some time to get them to sleep.

This can take some time for you to get them used to, but with less and less contact over time, you will be able to get the baby used to sleep on their own, and they will be able to fall asleep simply by being put in their bed at night.

Evaluating How the SWAP Is Going

Sometimes the plan is not going to go as smoothly as you would like and you may be convinced that you are now doomed. But as with any type of experiment that you do, some things are going to work and some things just won't work for you. Some days you will find that things go more smoothly for you than others. If you feel like SWAP is the best fit for you, then you need to commit to it for at least five to seven days before seeing results. Mastering a new skill is going to take time and some commitment, but if you stick with it, you are going to see the results. Some of the signs that you are on the right track and that this is the right plan for you include:

- *You find that bedtime is now a more enjoyable activity that all participants will enjoy.*

- *Your child is able to sleep for a longer period of time with fewer interruptions.*

- *Your child will stay asleep in the exact location that you put them in all night long.*

- *You are starting to feel confident enough to work on these strategies even during naps. Or, if you have already done them to work on naps, you find that the naptime is getting longer or your child is able to fall asleep much easier at nap.*

- *You are already moving towards a solid age appropriate night sleep and feeding schedule.*

However, these plans are not always going to work for every family. If you committed yourself consistently to SWAP for a week or more, and some of the things below are not true for you, it may be time to re-evaluate your plan and figure out if you are doing it right, or if you need to try out a different method to get your results. Some of the reasons that your plan may not be working for you include:

- It is not the right strategy for your baby. Each baby is different and one of the strategies above may not be right.

- You are not being consistent. You have to be consistent all of the time, or you are not going to see the results that you want.

- You got stalled. You may have started out with all of the best intentions to change up things during bedtime, but then you got scared. Instead of continuing, you made some smaller changes and then stop. You don't want to hang out around here if you want to see some results with getting your baby to sleep.

- A growth spurt, regression, illness, or travel came up and you weren't able to get the results. This happens, but you just need to reset the clock and start again. Try to pick out a time to try these techniques when none of the above is going on.

When you have put in your best efforts to implement a SWAP and it is a huge mess, then this is not a good plan for you and it is time to stop. While these are great plans that can help you get your baby to sleep, some babies are not going to respond well to them. And no matter how good a plan may be, if your baby doesn't respond to them, then they are not the right one for you. Sometimes it's just because the plan is not the right one for the baby, and sometimes it is because the baby is too young. If your child is between the ages of two months to four months, it may be time to push the pause button and come back to try it out later. Or, the problem is that SWAP is not the right option for you. That's okay, we have plenty of other methods that you can try out to help your baby sleep through the night.

Chapter 7:
Sleep Learning Independence Plan (SLIP)

In the last chapter, we focused a lot on working with gradual strategies that could help your baby become an independent sleeper. These strategies are often effective for most parents and they are usually a good place to start. However, there are some circumstances where these strategies aren't going to work that well for you and for your baby. Some of the reasons that these SWAP strategies may not work well include:

- Sleep is so bad for the baby that slowly working on it for a few weeks is not a good option.

- Your emotional and physical reserves are on empty. The SWAP strategies can be great, but you do need to have some energy in reserves to work on them.

- You have already tried doing some of the SWAP methods and they aren't successful for you.

Another option that you may want to try out is to sleep train without parental assistance. This can be known by a few different names including the CIO, cry it out, or Ferberizing. Fundamentally, they are all going to come down to placing the baby into a space that is safe for them when it is time to go to sleep, and then letting them figure out how to fall asleep on their own. This is going to involve quite a few tears and many parents are not fond of the cry it out methods.

There are a lot of people who are against the crying it out methods. They think that all that crying can be hard on the baby, that it can make the baby feel abandoned, and that it will result in long-term issues for the baby. Plus, some parents find that they have trouble listening to the crying for very long; and some kids can keep that crying up for a very long time.

Whether or not you decide to use a cry it out a plan with your child, it is going to depend on various factors. If the temperament of your child is right for this one, you may only have to do it a few times and the baby will go to sleep. If you have tried out some of the other methods and they didn't work, then this might be something to try. And you need to make sure that your own nerves are able to handle it as well. There are also some babies who can seemingly cry for hours on end. These cry it out methods is probably not the best option for them.

Should I SLIP or Not?
The next question that you may have about this sleep learning independence plan is whether or not to use them. The whole point of working with this plan is to teach the baby how to sleep on their own, without the help of the parent, because the involvement of the parent isn't working anymore and it may even be hindering how well the baby can establish their own healthy sleep

schedule. SLIP is more of a mindful parenting strategy that is used to help older babies to sleep on their own without having the parent nearby. They can generally involve some tears or complaints during the process, and these techniques work well for families who have not had much success with using the SWAP techniques that we talked about before or for whom severe sleep deprivation is causing issues right now.

At this point, you may be curious as to whether SLIP is the right technique for your family. Here is a checklist that you can go through to help you reach the conclusion on whether to use this or not. If you are able to answer yes to most of these questions, then it is probably time to start using SLIP.

Is the Baby At Least Six Months Old?

For younger babies, you can use some of the sleeping tools that we talked about before. SLIP generally works better with older children but take into account the temperament of your child to determine if these will work for them as well.

The Baby Has Chronic Issues with Sleep Deprivation.

IF your baby is getting quite a bit less sleep than they should, or they wake up a bunch of times during the night, then the baby is probably sleep deprived.

The Issue Here Is the Lack of Independent Sleep.

The SLIP technique is to help ingrain independent sleep in the baby. It can sometimes be applied to night weaning or even to early waking but it is going to work to deal with the baby's inability to fall asleep on their own.

Everything Else Hasn't Worked.
SLIP is often used as a last resort because it isn't as gentle on the baby as the other methods.

The Baby Isn't Suffering from Some Medical Complications.
Reflux, fevers, and colds can really make it hard to get the baby to sleep on their own. Consider waiting until after the issue is fixed before starting.

Baby Is in A Safe Space.
Make sure that the baby is left in a safe place when implementing SLIP. This can include their crib.

Both You and Your Partner Agree to Do This.
This is going to be a tough few days, so there isn't time for the two of you to fight over it. If you are still fighting with your partner about sleep, then don't get started with SLIP.

You Are Able to Maintain A Schedule That Is Consistent During That Time.

Sleep training is not something that you try to do the weekend before a big holiday. Find at least a few weeks when you can stick with a consistent schedule.

You Have A Good Night Vision Monitor.

If you don't have this, it doesn't mean that you can't work with SLIP, but it does help. It can help you to tell if the baby is asleep without walking into their room and risking them waking up on you.

You Are Committed.

You must be fully committed here. Your baby is going to try and get you to come back in and hold them and get them to sleep. If you do this, then you are going to send a mixed message and you will never get them to do this sleep technique.

How to Implement SLIP at Night

As with the SWAP technique that we talked about in the previous chapter, SLIP is going to work best if you try it at night because the child will already be biologically set up to go to sleep at night. There are a few things that need to happen in order to make the SLIP technique work for you.

The first step is to make sure that you get the baby down for naps using any means necessary. You do not want the child to be overly tired when it is time to go to bed at night. It doesn't matter which method you use at this point:

the car, a stroller, or rocking with you. For the next few days, make sure that you get those naps. You can work on independent sleeping at naptime later. Let's just focus on getting them to sleep independently at night for now. With that said, avoid those catnaps. These are cheating naps and won't give your baby the quality rest they need.

You can keep up with that consistent bedtime routine. This is a good way to help soothe the baby into sleep without having to do all of the work or all the nursing and cuddling. If you do nurse them before bed, which is fine, you just need to change up the order sometimes. For example, if your bedtime routine was a bath, books, boob, and then the bed, you would have to change it to boob, bath, books, and bed so that the baby doesn't get used to falling asleep while eating.

If the baby is swaddled during this time, it is fine to keep up with it, as long as you know they can't or they won't flip over. If you feel that the baby could potentially flip over at some time, then you should avoid swaddling while you are sleep training. If your child uses a pacifier and sleeps all night with it, this can eventually cause some sleep association problems that you will have to work on.

Before you get started with this method, make sure that the sleep location you choose for the baby is as safe as possible. Setting them down in their own crib is the best option, but also check out for other hazards. Are there any dangling cords the baby can reach? Can the baby climb out of the crib or fall out? Is the crib clear of any hazards like pillows, bumpers, blankets, or stuffed animals? Does the crib or any other furniture present a tip over hazard that you need to work with?

Make sure that from here, the baby is put down to sleep at the right bedtime. This should be the time that the child was historically falling asleep in the past. The key word here is sleep. If you spent an hour rocking the baby to sleep every night before they went out, then the bedtime would not be at the time when you began the rocking. It would be when the baby was asleep. This is going to be your new bedtime so get comfortable.

If you say anything to the baby before you leave the room, or before bedtime, then you need to be consistent with it here. Your baby is going to be very receptive to language and they will understand what you are saying, even if they aren't able to speak it themselves. Say something positive that helps explain what is going on without making the baby feel worried. Be firm, loving, and consistent in this.

After the bedtime routine is done and the room is safe and comfy, lay the baby down in their own bed before leaving the room. There are some strategies here that will have you camp out in the room because having your presence there can be helpful in the soothing process. However, many parents find that the opposite is true and them being in the room can make the baby more upset because they want to be picked up and cuddled. It can also create an issue with object permanence where the baby will come to expect that you will sit there in the room when they wake up at night, and when you aren't there, it can cause some issues.

If one of the parents is going to have more trouble with this process than the other, then it may be time to send one of them away. Letting them sit in the hallway or near the door and hear the crying, and feel guilty at the same time, can be detrimental to how well this process would go. That parent is the one who will give in and all the hard work will be lost. Sometimes this is the mom and other times it can be a dad. Whoever it may be, consider sending them outside or to another part of the house so the crying doesn't bother them as much.

After you lay the baby down for the night, give them some time to figure out how they are going to fall asleep without you. The baby may be sad, furious, angry, or even a combination of things. Ask yourself some questions here. Is the baby safe, fed, and loved? If you can answer yes to these, then you have done your job. From here, the baby is working on something that is new and it frustrates them. While it can be hard to listen to, it is fine for the baby to feel frustrated sometimes.

With this method, don't give up! Have faith that your child is going to be able to figure this out and that they will learn how to sleep without you. No, the baby is not going to want to, and they won't make it easy. But your baby has the ability to do this just fine. Going in now is just going to sabotage your goal of improving sleep and if you give in, it guarantees that the next time is worse. Just keep strong and it will get better.

Should I Check in or Not?

SLIP is based on the idea that your child must learn how to sleep without any unsustainable sleep associations. Typically, if you are the one who provides that sleep association in the form of cuddling, feeding, nursing, or rocking, then it is not going to be good if you go and check in on the baby. If they are still awake, the baby will expect that you are going to provide them with the sleep association that they are looking for.

When you fail to provide this, which you should fail to do this if you are fully committed to not going back to your old way of doing things, the baby is not going to be happy and they will be furious. They are used to doing things a certain way and you are not going along with the plan which can make the baby very unhappy.

For most babies, if you go back into the room to check on them, this is going to make things more difficult. This is why the full extinction method is the best one if you want to make SLIP work. For this one, you will place the child down while they are fully awake, making sure they are comfortable and safe, and then you don't return until after they are asleep.

There are also other SLIP methods that go against this plan. For example, Dr. Ferber suggested a method that is more of a graduated extinction. This method has the parent go back in for some brief checks at progressively longer intervals. You would start going in after three minutes, then after five more minutes, and then after ten minutes. With this approach, your child will probably cry horribly throughout each visit. Regardless, you will go in to make sure they are safe and then remind them that it is time for them to go to sleep before leaving the room again.

There is evidence that shows how both the graduated and the full extinction method are effective when it comes to improving sleep outcomes. But there isn't any evidence that shows how one is better than the other. Most parents seem to enjoy graduated extinction more because they feel that checking in periodically is more loving to the baby. There isn't really evidence to support that this is the better method, but if it makes you feel better while using the cry it out method, then go for it.

If you do decide to make a brief visit into your child during these methods, the five-minute plan may be the best one to try out. There is not really an ideal schedule when it comes to checking in on the baby during SLIP, but there are some key elements that should be present to make the graduated extinction plan work for you:

- It is simple so there are no user errors.

- Each interval ends up being longer than the previous ones.

- These intervals need to be long enough so that your child has a chance to fall asleep on their own.

Any schedule of visits that can meet these criteria will work just fine. Make it work for your needs. With the five-minute plan, you go in at five minutes, then go in ten minutes after the first visit, and then fifteen minutes after the second visit and on down the line until the baby falls asleep. When you go into the room, you do not pick up the child but spend time reiterating the soothing words that were used during bedtime. And make sure that you leave the room before the baby falls asleep.

Watch Out for The Extinction Burst
For most babies, the SLIP method is going to have a few nights that are challenging for the parents and then there is a dramatic and immediate improvement in how they sleep. There are other babies who will continue to cry longer and louder. You may find that you are not so confident in SLIP and how it can work for your baby. Or maybe you were successful with SLIP and then after a few weeks you find that your happy baby is up and crying again. If the latter has happened to you, then you are going through what is known as the extinction burst.

SLIP is often known as an extinction therapy that has the parent work to make any undesirable behavior, in this case, sleep, become extinct because you no longer reinforce or reward the behavior. And for about seventy percent of the parents who try it, this method is effective. They will spend a few days up to a week working on getting their baby to sleep at night and listening to the baby cry during that time. But once the week is over, the baby will be able to get put into bed and fall asleep without all the fighting and crying any longer.

However, for the remaining parents, the baby is going to start aping up on how much they cry. Or they may take a break for a few days from the crying and then they resume the crying again. This resumption is going to be known as an extinction burst where the child is doing even more of the behavior that you are trying to extinguish now that you took the reinforcer away. What can you do about this? Nothing really. You just have to stick with the plan and ride it all out until it is done.

The only thing that you can do here is to wait it out and hope that it ends before you lose your mind. And this is probably why these SLIP methods have just a bad reputation in the long term. They may work for some parents but others just can't deal with the weeks of going through all the crying. Sure, it will get better, but it can be hard on the nerves even if it doesn't require a lot of involvement from the parent.

This is why you need to carefully choose the sleep method that you want to use in your family. Many people go with the SWAP methods because, yes, they do need to be involved, but at least it doesn't require hours of crying to get the baby to sleep. SLIP can work well for a lot of parents and after a few days, the crying will be done and you will have a baby who can fall asleep on their own. But, if the baby doesn't fall asleep, and keeps going on with this trend, it can make for some very long nights.

Picking which of these sleep methods you want to go with can sometimes be a challenge. They both have pretty high success rates, and they can both works based on your baby and what they are like. You may have to experiment with a few different options to see which one is the best for you and for your baby. And you must remember that no matter how good the method may be, it is never going to work overnight.

Chapter 8:
If Night Waking Starts to Happen Again?

If you have gotten to this part of the guidebook, then congratulations! You have successfully used either SLIP or SWAP to help foster some independent sleep patterns in your baby, at least during bedtime. Some parents may have even gone so far as to move these techniques over to nap time as well. You have taught your child a very important life skill!

Chances are after you are successful with these techniques; you are going to see a dramatic and immediate reduction in the number of times the baby is up and moving during the night, especially if you used some of the sleeping tools that we discussed before. This is a big win for you as a parent so go ahead and celebrate a little bit.

This, however, isn't the end of the story. SLIP and SWAP are all about being able to fall asleep independently without any unsustainable sleep associations. However, they are not always a free pass to getting the baby to completely sleep through the night. You have created a possibility for the child to sleep through the night, but there are still going to be some night waking during this time.

It is not time to come up with a plan to address these extra awake times at night. And the plan that you come up with is going to be very dependent on the reason that your child is waking up in the first place. There are usually two main reasons why your baby is still waking up at night even after using SLIP and SWAP. These reasons include:

- They are hungry and need food.

- They lost their sleep association such as a pacifier, cuddling, or rocking.

- Let's take a look at each of these and explore what you can do to try and eliminate the baby waking up so many times during the night.

Waking and Eating
If your baby was routinely eating during the night before sleep training, then they are going to either expect or need to do this even after you have established the independent sleep. If you did this sleep training with a younger baby, they may not have reached the right developmental stage to go all night without needing food. If you did this with an older baby, they may be capable of going a long time without eating but they are used to these night feedings and it may take some time to shift their calories all over to the daylight hours.

For a child who is nursing, it is sometimes hard to know how much food they have taken in. Some are able to guzzle a ton of milk in just a few minutes; some will take a few minutes just to get things going. And some will get more than others. It isn't always an easy formula to get how much they eat from how long they nurse because this will vary for each baby.

Sometimes it is easier when the baby will take a bottle simply because you know exactly how much they are consuming at all points of the day. Maybe your baby is only drinking a few ounces for each feeding but then they demand many bottles throughout the night. Or maybe the baby is able to guzzle down a few large bottles. If you know how much they are taking in, you can consider the total volume consumed at night as a percentage of daily intake.

Let's say that your six-month-old takes in about 28 ounces of formula a day and then wake up four times at night to drink two ounces each time. Even though the individual feedings are pretty small, over the total of the night, she is taking in eight ounces, or about 30 percent of her intake.

Regardless of the age of your baby, if they are eating often or they camp on the boob all night, you can and should assume that they are consuming a substantial amount of food. And if you still aren't sure if your baby is eating a lot during the night, some of the other signs you can look for include:

- Having to change the diaper a few times at night to avoid big leaks.
- The morning diaper is so full that it is falling off and can't hold anymore.
- The baby isn't starving for food when they first wake up in the morning.

If you are doing sleep training with a younger baby, you will just need to feed them during these times. They are used to getting those calories at night and will just wake up more if you don't provide them to the baby. Just make sure that you don't let the baby fall asleep while holding onto the bottle or nursing. This will just bring out that sleep association again and can make things difficult down the road. Feed the baby until they are full and then when they are still a little bit awake, you can lay them back down in the crib and leave.

If your baby is a little bit older, it may be time to start minimizing their intake and their meals during the night and moving these feedings to other times. Make sure that the baby is well fed (don't overdo it or they may have an upset stomach) but make sure that they have enough they won't be hungry a few hours later. As they start to move to solids and more substantial foods, the baby should be able to go most, if not all, of the night without needing to eat. If they still act like they need a lot of food during this time, it may just be the fact that they have sleep association with the bottle or the breast, and you need to work on breaking that habit.

Baby Wakes Up but Is Not Hungry
There are sometimes other reasons that the baby will wake up at night besides being hungry. The first reason may be that the baby hasn't quite mastered the art of going back into their deep sleep mode without your assistance. While you have done a great job of taking those first steps to remove yourself from bedtime, there is a chance that your baby is going to keep waking up periodically for the first few nights, and maybe even longer, expecting you to go back to those behaviors they are used to.

Being able to establish these independent sleep patterns means that you need to be steadfast and not do whatever habit you did before using SLIP or SWAP. While the baby may wish that you would go back and do them again, giving in is going to ruin all your hard work and can make it hard to keep the baby to sleep. Yes, the baby may fuss for a bit but they will adjust and soon they will sleep through the night.

In general, you should handle all the nighttime awakenings that are unrelated to food in the same way that you handled bedtime. If you are working on the SLIP method, you should let the baby navigate these periods independently. You know that they are able to do this since they showed you how they could fall asleep on their own during bed. It just may take a few days before they can get into a routine of falling asleep on their own.

On the other hand, if you chose a SWAP method, you may need to go back into the room and finish that. For example, some parents will rub their baby's back to help them fall asleep with the SWAP method. If this is what you did, then when the baby wakes up again at night and isn't hungry, you will go back in there and rub their back to get them to sleep.

In addition to that information, you may want to consider some of the following guidelines as well:

- If it has only been a few hours since you put the baby down to bed, you should give them some time to resettle down on their own. The compulsion for the baby to just fall back asleep during this time can be potent and sometimes your intervention is going to reinforce their waking. If you give your child some space, they may fall right back to sleep.

- When your child wakes up, your decision tree will rely on two options. The first one is that you go over to your child after giving them five to ten minutes to try and fall asleep on their own. The second is to just wait it out until the baby goes back to sleep without your assistance.

- If you are convinced that your baby is waking up and that you need to interfere, then you must repeat the process that was used during bedtime. As a general rule, before midnight, you will want to have your child go back to sleep without you. But after you get past midnight, it is fine to offer a bit of assistance.

- You should remember to be really stingy when you try to help your child fall asleep during the night. You are changing things up and this is hard for the baby at first but they can handle it. Remember that each time you run into the room to cuddle or bounce your child, you are rewarding them for waking up. We are not trying to be mean here, just trying to make sure that the baby will fall asleep and stay asleep.

- Commit to being less involved each night. This helps the baby adjust to you not doing all the work. For example, if you spent twenty minutes patting their back on one night to get them to sleep, commit to only patting their back for fifteen minutes the next one.

How to Deal with Wakeups Early in The Morning

The biological compulsion to stay asleep is very strong for babies in the evening at bedtime but it does kind of peter out when you get closer to the morning. Many babies are going to wake up early in the morning such as at four or five in the morning simply because their sleep drive is pretty low during this point.

If the baby does wake up at an incredibly early hour, the first thing you may want to try is to see if SWAP or SLIP will be enough to help them get back to sleep until a better time. This is not always going to work for you though. You may have to try it for a few weeks to see but because the compulsion to stay asleep is so low during the morning, it may not work out the way that you want and the baby may want to wake up.

Many parents have found success by giving their baby a quick snack during these early hours. This can help give everyone a few more hours of sleep. Doing this for an hour or so during the morning to give everyone a break is generally not going to ruin all the work that you did all night when it comes to independent sleep. So, go ahead and give them something to eat and maybe spend a few minutes cuddling with them to get them back. Over time, they will learn how to sleep independently, especially if you have kept up with all of the other sleep training techniques that we have talked about.

One thing to remember here is that the goal of independent sleep is not night weaning. Typically, the number of requests that you get at night from the baby to eat is going to diminish quite a bit as they grow older and independent sleep is established. But in the beginning, your child may demand to eat a few times during the night. After some time, as your baby can take in more food during the day and gets on a better schedule, you may decide that it is time to get rid of one or two feedings during the night, and eventually, you will decide to fully night wean the baby.

No matter how well you do with SLIP or SWAP, there are still going to be times when your baby is going to wake up at night. Often this is because they are hungry and you simply need to feed them and they will go back to sleep. Don't fret too much about this. As the baby gets older and gets on a routine with SLIP or SWAP, they will start sleeping completely through the night.

Chapter 9:
How to Handle Naptime Troubles

After you have had some time to sleep train your baby during bedtime, it is time to move on and help your baby prepare to sleep during naptimes. Many parents still struggle with this time even after they have been able to get their baby to sleep during the night. Babies of all ages still need to have some quiet time, as well as a naptime, to help them get enough rest during the day. But some children are going to fight against this. Let's take a look at some of the things you should know in order to get started with sleep training during nap time.

When Should Naptime Training Start?
There are three options that you can choose when it comes to nap training. Some parents choose to do the nap training and night training at the same time. They think that because they are already doing the work for one, they may as well do it for both. It can be a bit painful and a big hassle when you are doing them, but it can help maintain consistency and will eliminate any confusion the baby may have. It takes some work, but it can be done if you are consistent and ready for the challenge.

Another option is to do nap training first. Parents who choose this option prefer to work with the naps first and do a test run to see how it all works. However, this is not always the best option. You will find that while babies may automatically fall into a pattern of good naps once you establish a good bedtime sleep, it doesn't go the other way. This means that you may have to do the work twice to get both bedtime and naptime to work for you.

If you are going to do the nap time and bedtime sleep training separately, then you should start with night training first. This is a longer period of time you need the baby to sleep during, and if you can get the baby to sleep through the night, it means that you can finally get the rest that you need. Then, once the baby can sleep through the night, you can handle naptime with a bit more energy.

How to Do Nap Training

If you have already started with a bedtime sleep training routine, and it has worked well for you, then there is no reason why you can't keep this up now that you are moving on to nap time. It is best to stick with the same sleeping techniques if possible because this can avoid a lot of confusion when it comes to your baby falling asleep at night and when it is time to take a nap.

The first thing you need to keep in mind when working on nap time, outside of using the same technique as bedtime, is to follow the natural schedule of your baby. While there are times when this may get messed up such as for vacations or if you had a rocky night of sleep, you want to try to follow the natural rhythms of your baby. Some babies want to take three smaller naps during the day while others will take two bigger naps. Trying to force the baby to take more naps than they naturally want to do can lead to a lot of hard work for you. Follow some of the cues that your baby gives you and work from there to come up with a sleep schedule that works for both of you.

Another thing to remember is that you should never have the last nap be too close to bedtime. It isn't going to work well if your baby is waking up from their nap at six at night, and then you want to get them to bed at seven. The baby, no matter what age, is going to need a good chunk of time between their last nap and when you want them to fall asleep, or they will simply have too much energy to fall asleep. If you want them to bed by seven, the last nap should probably end no later than four, and maybe earlier if the child is a little bit older.

Before laying the baby down for a nap, do some of the same things that you would do for the baby at bedtime. Make sure that you have played with them and gotten them worn out a bit. This can include playing with toys, free play, and spending time outside. Make sure that they have had time to eat as well so they won't wake up hungry later. You can also change them, make sure their clothes and bed are comfy, and that they have everything they need for a safe and comfortable nap time.

When you lay the baby down, it is best to use the same techniques that you use for bedtime training. This includes bringing in some of the sleep tools that we discussed earlier in this guidebook. These sleep tools can sometimes be enough to lull the baby to a good nap time without any added work, provided that you did a good job with sleep training at night. You may need to put in a little bit extra work to get them to fall asleep during nap time than you do with bedtime, but it won't take long to get them ready.

Nap time doesn't have to be a big hassle with your baby. If you have implemented a good sleep schedule with them and you have worked to get your chosen sleep training technique to work for your baby at night time, then nap time won't take a lot of added effort on your part.

Chapter 10:
Common Setbacks

While you may have the best intentions when you get started with sleep training, there are times when your baby is not going to go along with the plan that you have set out. They may have anxiety about being separated from you, may run into trouble when you are on vacation, and so much more. Let's look at some of the common setbacks that you may experience during this time and what you can do to prevent it from ruining all your efforts.

Sleep Regression

Every once in a while, no matter how good you are at setting up a sleep schedule with your baby, their sleep will all of a sudden become a big mess. At this time, the baby is going to become fussy as well, which can either be the cause or the result of this sleep deprivation.

Sleep regression can be hard on a parent, but it is perfectly normal in most cases. If the sleep regression is happening because the baby is going through new milestones, going through a growth spurt, or suffering from something like teething, then take heart. They will be over it soon and things will get back to normal.

But, if the sleep regression occurs because you have gotten lax on your sleep training methods and you are just letting the baby sleep however they want, then this can be a problem. You have to maintain the work that you did during sleep training to get the full benefits and to ensure random sleep regressions don't occur to you.

Separation Anxiety

Baby separation anxiety is when the baby fears that when you leave, they are never going to see you again. This can be either when you leave them with another person, or when you go out of the room. Sometimes, it is when the baby wakes up and night and notices that you are no longer there. Observing this behavior can be heartbreaking but take note that it is an important developmental stage for your baby. Through this process, they will learn how to be an independent person.

Separation anxiety is often going show up when the baby is about four to six months and then will peak when the baby is about twelve to eighteen months old. There are some babies who will still suffer from separation anxiety when they are two.

When the baby is first born, they don't know any better. They think that they will never be separated from you. However, at this age, they won't really remember that you exist when it is time to leave the room because they just don't understand how object permanence works. But when the baby reaches four to six months, they are going to learn that you and they are different beings. They will also remember you, even if they are not able to see you. However, at this age, the baby doesn't have the sense of time, nor do they have the experience to know that you will come back soon. To them, they think you will be gone forever.

Feeling anxious is pretty normal for them because they don't feel your security-inducing presence around any longer. You can probably guess that babies who have a lot of separation anxiety near bedtime are ones who will be really hard to settle down for the night. And they will have a ton of trouble self-soothing when they wake up at night.

So, how can you avoid these issues with separation anxiety and your baby? A few things that you can try out will include:

Play Some Games Like Hide and Seek and Peek-A-Boo.
When the baby is only a few months old, start playing these games. You can slowly hide for a bit longer each time. When the baby learns that you will reappear each time this happens, they will quickly learn that you will be back, even during times when they don't see you.

Talk About What You Plan to Do.
You will be surprised at how much babies are able to understand. This is why it is a good idea to let them know what you plan to do when you leave. This helps them to feel less scared.

Don't Dramatize.
It may be hard to leave your baby, especially when they are dealing with separation anxiety but you must act like it is not a big deal. The baby will take their cues from you. If you act like your leaving isn't that big of a deal, then the baby will start to learn that as well.

Share Your Tasks with Another Caretaker.
If it is possible, have someone else help take the baby to bed. This can help the baby get used to the idea that you won't always be doing that for them. Of course, this is harder when you are breastfeeding since you are the only one who can do this.

Keep Your Promises.
If you place the baby down and they seem nervous, let them know you will be back if they need you. Then come back. Keeping these promises can help the baby feel secure that you won't leave them.

Traveling
If you travel with a baby, just be prepared for some messed up sleeping patterns. This is true while you are gone and probably for a few days after you return. You are taking the baby away from what is familiar to them and they may be anxious and even distracted by all of the new things. It is hard for a lot of adults to stay on a sleep schedule when they travel, so imagine what it must feel like to a little baby who is just getting used to their sleep schedule.

There are a few things that you can do to make sure that your baby is able to sleep well even when you are traveling. Some of the things that you can try out include:

Bring Something That They See as Familiar from Home.
This can make it easier for the baby to fall asleep. It can be the white noise sound they are used to, a stuffed animal, or a favorite blanket, anything that is going to help your baby fall asleep.

Don't Be Too Worried About the Baby Sleeping Outside.
If you are on a vacation, the last thing that you should worry about is having to head somewhere for naptime. Bring along something that is breathable and can go over the stroller and let the baby sleep there. If your baby is able to fall asleep in the stroller at their regular naptime, this is just fine.

Bring A Travel Cot or Someplace Else for The Baby to Sleep.
Even if you are not at home, it is best for the baby to sleep in their own space. Bring along something for the baby to sleep in, or call ahead to your hotel to see if they can provide you with something. Then, when it is time for bed, just follow your regular bedtime and lay the baby down using the same techniques that you used at home.

Don't Get Started with Any New Bad Sleep Habits at This Time.

Just because you are not at home doesn't mean that you should start up some new sleeping habits with the baby. For example, if you don't share a bed with the baby at home, then there really isn't a reason to start this habit when you are on vacation. If you don't rock the baby to sleep at home, then don't do it on vacation. Sure, you will probably have to spend a little longer getting the baby to sleep because of the new location, but stick with what you usually do so that your baby doesn't develop new habits that you have to break later on.

Change in The Time (Daylight Saving Time)

When the time changes during Daylight Saving Time, it can be a nightmare for families, no matter what age their child is. They worry that the time change is going to mess with the sleep training that they have worked so hard on. The baby is not used to this time change but since everything now operates on this new time change, it is important to get the baby moved over. And it happens two times a year!

The best thing to do with this is to gently move bedtime just a little bit at a time. When the time moves forward or backward, slowly move the bedtime fifteen minutes at a time, in either direction that you need. This isn't such a big change that it is going to ruin all your work but gets the baby on the new time schedule within a week or so.

Unfortunately, there's nothing that you can do to stop the time change, and it is something that every parent has to go through. But with a little planning, and realizing that you may have a few rough nights, you will be able to get the baby on the new schedule.

Your Child Doesn't Nap

Most babies are going to take a nap during the day. They may not take them at the times that you want and sometimes they may not last as long as you would like but most babies can't go more than a few hours without needing to take a nap of some kind. This is a good thing for a parent who needs a break; however, as your child reaches toddler age, they may go through times when they refuse to take a nap. It doesn't matter if mom and dad are exhausted and need a break, and it doesn't matter if the toddler is tired and needs to fall asleep, sometimes they are going to refuse to nap.

If this only happens a few days here and there, it isn't a big deal. But when your child is throwing a tantrum on the floor because they are so exhausted for skipping their naps, you will naturally look for a solution to this issue. The art here comes in the form of using gentle coercion and using it to make a solid and predictable naptime.

While this may sound simple in theory, it can be a struggle. Many families struggle with this and often it is not that big of a deal, other than the parents need a break if the toddler gets enough sleep during the night. To help you determine whether naps are completely gone from your life forever, or if you are just hitting a bump in the road, the two questions that you need to ask right now are how many hours is the child sleeping at night, and are these hours enough.

When we talk about children who are between the ages of two and four, they will need somewhere between 11 to 15 hours of sleep during the day. This is a big spectrum and it will vary based on the child at hand. If your child is on the latter end of this range, your child is probably not going to fight with taking a nap. However, some toddlers will only need the eleven hours at night and it is very rare that they will take a nap.

Now, if we are talking about a baby, you may have to still try to convince them to take a nap. You can utilize some of the sleep training techniques that we have been talking about in the rest of this guidebook to help you gently lull the baby to sleep. And just like how it happened when you did sleep training in the evening and at bedtime, you may have to spend a few days to make this happen.

Even with an older child, you still need to give them some downtime even if they aren't napping. This can be good to calm the child down and can ensure that you also get a break. You can have the child to sit in their room with a few books or some coloring pages and tell them that they must sit in their rooms and be quiet for a bit. Some kids will start to doze off anyway but when the child gets some say in the process, but you still get a little break.

Starting the Day Too Early
Keep in mind that all babies are going to wake up too early, way earlier than the parents would pick if they had a choice. The only question is whether the time is too early for the parent or if it is actually too early for the baby. Babies

are going to usually wake up early, often sometime between six and six-thirty in the morning. Some make it even earlier.

Your goal needs to be maximizing the total amount of uninterrupted sleep that your child gets during the night. For most babies, this will be about eleven hours of sleep at night. But there are some babies who are neither getting ten or eleven hours of sleep and they also aren't making it to six in the morning. If your baby is legitimately getting up too early, there are a few things that you can try to get them to stay asleep including:

Make Bedtime Earlier.
Some babies are going to bed too late and this can make them cranky. When they are fussy, they may have a hard time falling asleep and staying asleep in the morning. It may seem counterintuitive but sometimes putting the baby to bed a little bit earlier will get them to sleep later in the day. You can test this out. Try putting them into bed a little earlier for about three to five days and see if it works.

If your baby gets their ten to eleven hours of sleep by four in the morning, it is going to be pretty hard to convince them to go back to bed. You may need to make the bedtime a little later and that could solve the whole problem.

You may need to spend some time experimenting here to see what works the best for the baby and for the parents. You can start out with a later bedtime and see if that solves the problem. If you feel that the baby is getting enough sleep by the time they wake up, then this may be the choice to go with. However, if they aren't getting the ten to eleven hours and are still getting up early, consider moving the bedtime a little earlier and see if that works for you.

Conclusion

Thanks for making it through to the end of *Baby Sleep Training*. Let's hope it was informative and able to provide you with all of the tools you need to achieve your goals whatever they may be.

The next step is to utilize some of these methods for your own. Many parents run into trouble when it comes to helping their babies get to sleep. They want to make sure that their baby is getting plenty of shut-eye at night but they also want to be able to do something other than holding the baby the whole night. The techniques that we discussed in this guidebook will help you to finally get your baby to be an independent sleeper.

There are many different techniques that you can choose when it comes to sleep training. You may have to try a few different techniques in order to get your baby to sleep. But with some patience, and by following these techniques, you will be able to get that baby to sleep!

If you find this book helpful in anyway a review to support my endeavors is much appreciated.

Heidi Oster

www.ingramcontent.com/pod-product-compliance
Lightning Source LLC
Chambersburg PA
CBHW060459080526
44584CB00015B/1488